THE TWELVE DAYS OF CHRISTMAS

THE TWELVE DAYS OF CHRISTMAS

ILLUSTRATED BY ILSE PLUME

Harper & Row, Publishers

The Twelve Days of Christmas
Copyright © 1990 by Ilse Plume
Printed in the U.S.A. All rights reserved.
Design by Ilse Plume
1 2 3 4 5 6 7 8 9 10
First Edition

Library of Congress Cataloging-in-Publication Data
Twelve days of Christmas (English folk song)
    The twelve days of Christmas / illustrated by Ilse Plume.
        p.   cm.
    Summary: A favorite song of the Christmas season, illustrated,
with musical arrangement included.
    ISBN 0-06-024737-1 : $. — ISBN 0-06-024738-X (lib. bdg.) :
$
    1. Folk-songs, English—Texts.   2. Christmas music.   [1. Folk
songs, English.   2. Christmas music.]   I. Plume, Ilse, ill.
II. Title.
PZ8.3.T8517   89-49063
[P1 1990]   CIP
782.42'1723'00268—dc20   AC

To my family—
my daughter, Anne-Marie;
my mother, Alice;
and the memory of my father, Richard

ON THE FIRST DAY OF CHRISTMAS

My true love sent to me

A partridge in a pear tree.

ON THE SECOND DAY OF
CHRISTMAS

My true love sent to me

Two turtledoves

And a partridge in a pear tree.

ON THE THIRD DAY OF
CHRISTMAS

My true love sent to me

Three French hens,

Two turtledoves,

And a partridge in a pear tree.

ON THE FOURTH DAY OF
CHRISTMAS

My true love sent to me

Four calling birds,

Three French hens,

Two turtledoves,

And a partridge in a pear tree.

ON THE FIFTH DAY OF
CHRISTMAS

My true love sent to me

Five gold rings,

Four calling birds,

Three French hens,

Two turtledoves,

And a partridge in a pear tree.

ON THE SIXTH DAY OF
CHRISTMAS

My true love sent to me

Six geese a-laying,

Five gold rings,

Four calling birds,

Three French hens,

Two turtledoves,

And a partridge in a pear tree.

ON THE SEVENTH DAY OF
CHRISTMAS

My true love sent to me

Seven swans a-swimming,

Six geese a-laying,

Five gold rings,

Four calling birds,

Three French hens,

Two turtledoves,

And a partridge in a pear tree.

ON THE EIGHTH DAY OF
CHRISTMAS

My true love sent to me

Eight maids a-milking,

Seven swans a-swimming,

Six geese a-laying,

Five gold rings,

Four calling birds,

Three French hens,

Two turtledoves,

And a partridge in a pear tree.

ON THE NINTH DAY OF
CHRISTMAS

My true love sent to me

Nine drummers drumming,

Eight maids a-milking,

Seven swans a-swimming,

Six geese a-laying,

Five gold rings,

Four calling birds,

Three French hens,

Two turtledoves,

And a partridge in a pear tree.

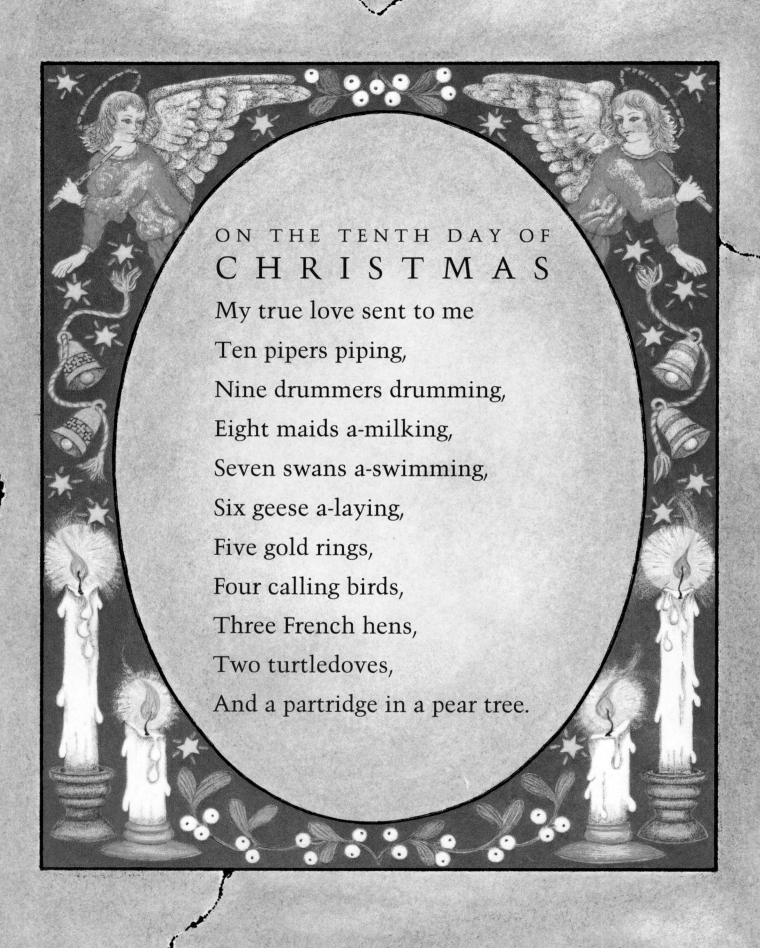

ON THE TENTH DAY OF
CHRISTMAS

My true love sent to me

Ten pipers piping,

Nine drummers drumming,

Eight maids a-milking,

Seven swans a-swimming,

Six geese a-laying,

Five gold rings,

Four calling birds,

Three French hens,

Two turtledoves,

And a partridge in a pear tree.

ON THE ELEVENTH DAY OF
CHRISTMAS
My true love sent to me

Eleven ladies dancing,

Ten pipers piping,

Nine drummers drumming,

Eight maids a-milking,

Seven swans a-swimming,

Six geese a-laying,

Five gold rings,

Four calling birds,

Three French hens,

Two turtledoves,

And a partridge in a pear tree.

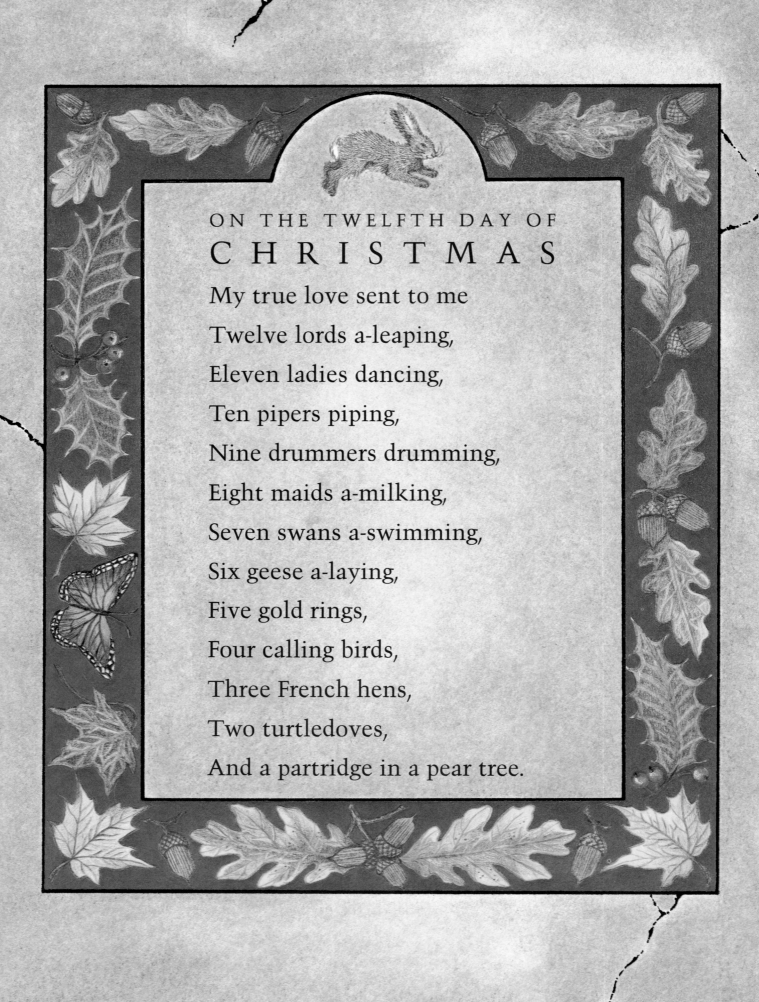

ON THE TWELFTH DAY OF
CHRISTMAS

My true love sent to me

Twelve lords a-leaping,

Eleven ladies dancing,

Ten pipers piping,

Nine drummers drumming,

Eight maids a-milking,

Seven swans a-swimming,

Six geese a-laying,

Five gold rings,

Four calling birds,

Three French hens,

Two turtledoves,

And a partridge in a pear tree.

The Twelve Days of Christmas

Arr. by Ray Kimmelman

ABOUT THE BOOK

I first began this project in 1985, although the seeds were already planted years before that when I came across a quotation by Robert Browning: "Open my heart and you will see/Graved inside of it, 'Italy.' " Twice in my life I have had the good fortune to live in Florence, "the cradle of the Renaissance." This was enough to infuse my soul with a touch of Tuscan sunlight forever.

My idea has been to convey the atmosphere, both tangible and intangible, of the Italian Renaissance. My goal has not been to duplicate existing manuscripts but rather to use them as a point of departure.

Over the years I have pored over numerous illuminated manuscripts, books of hours, miniatures, and bestiaries. I have used resources at the British Museum in London, the Metropolitan Museum (The Cloisters) and the Pierpont Morgan Library in New York, and the churches, libraries, and museums of Florence. I have visited monastic cells as well as Renaissance gardens in an effort to capture the essence of a particular time and place.

I hope that the reader, too, in walking through the pages of my book, will feel the sense of tranquility that he or she would have felt wandering through a Renaissance garden.

Ilse Plume